MW01715454

Magic Images

Eye Fun 3D

Steven Wilson & Marek Jacenko

Allbit Publishing
EyeFun3D.com

Table of Contents

Introduction	3
Viewing instructions	4
Eye Fun Images - Easiest to See	5
Eye Fun Images - Intermediate Level	12
Eye Fun Images - For the Best	27
Answers	32

CAUTION

Your mind might turn upside down.

Once you discover the three-dimensional Eye Fun images – great, eye-relaxing fun for people of all ages – you might just look at the world in a completely different way.

It is about your experience

This is the first volume of Magic 3D Images! A series of books **created for your entertainment and amusement**, but also to challenge you visually. The three-dimensional images will fascinate every time you view them.

The images in this book are designed to bring great pleasure and joy to your heart. It is amazing how surprising it can be every time a certain image jumps out at you. A full 3D effect without using any funny glasses.

Allow yourself to be enchanted by the beauty and technology used to create these Eye Fun creations, because you will never forget your first time!

Instructions

3D images can pose a difficult challenge (which is all part of the fun). It all adds to the tremendous satisfaction you feel once you do manage to see them.

Although possibly tricky at first, once you spot one 3D Eye Fun image you can almost get addicted. Look at each picture and check out what lies hidden within.

Your skills accelerate quickly and the images become much easier to see as you go along. These images within images are not only fun to look at, but also help you relax your eye muscles and improve your vision.

All the 3D images are sharp and can be seen clearly. There's no need to guess what things are hidden in them.

You can look at them if you wear glasses or contact lenses. It doesn't matter. But if you can, take off your glasses and look at the images without them. This will help your eyes relax and unwind even more.

Of course, seeing 3D images requires a little training and a lot of patience at the beginning, but the effort is paid back ten fold.

Believe it or not, you'll be able to see hidden 3D images in a matter of seconds, simply by looking at them.

The First and Last Rule *Relax*

It's strange how living in the modern world strains our eyes on a daily basis instead of relaxing them. A common mistake for beginners is to try and strain their eyes. This only causes tension. (Likely everyone who has not read this manual will start out that way.)

If you look at the hidden images correctly (just relax your eyes and mind), it helps to relieve eye strain and tiredness, and even improves your eyesight by relaxing your eye muscles.

Method 1

To see the 3D images, just let yourself drift off into a dreamy state of mind and gaze into the distance. Let your eyes and eye muscles relax. Holding the book in front of you, focus some distance beyond it and let the 3D image appear. It doesn't require any tension or forced concentration. Just let your eyes relax by looking into the distance and observe how the image appears.

Method 2

Find a reflection of light on the page or some refraction on the surface of the paper. Start to observe it, without any tension; simply look. You can even treat it as a short meditation exercise, allowing your thoughts to flow freely. This reflection or refraction of light will help you see the 3D image.

Method 3

Open the book at the page with the image you want to see and bring it closer and closer your eyes until it touches your nose. Then slowly move it away from you to a normal reading distance.

Observe the image, but without straining your eyes. Seeing a 3D image emerge from a randomly coloured pattern for the first time is a magical moment indeed.

These images give joy, although they do require some effort at first. It might take a few tries before you see anything, so if you don't succeed immediately, keep going because the prize is worth it in the end.

When you finally have the opportunity to see Eye Fun images, you'll discover a whole new dimension of reality. This entire collection of 28 images may keep you occupied for a few hours as you relax your eyes and mind, looking at each page until the image appears.

You will become an Eye Fun Champion in no time at all.

Relax your eyes.
Have fun!

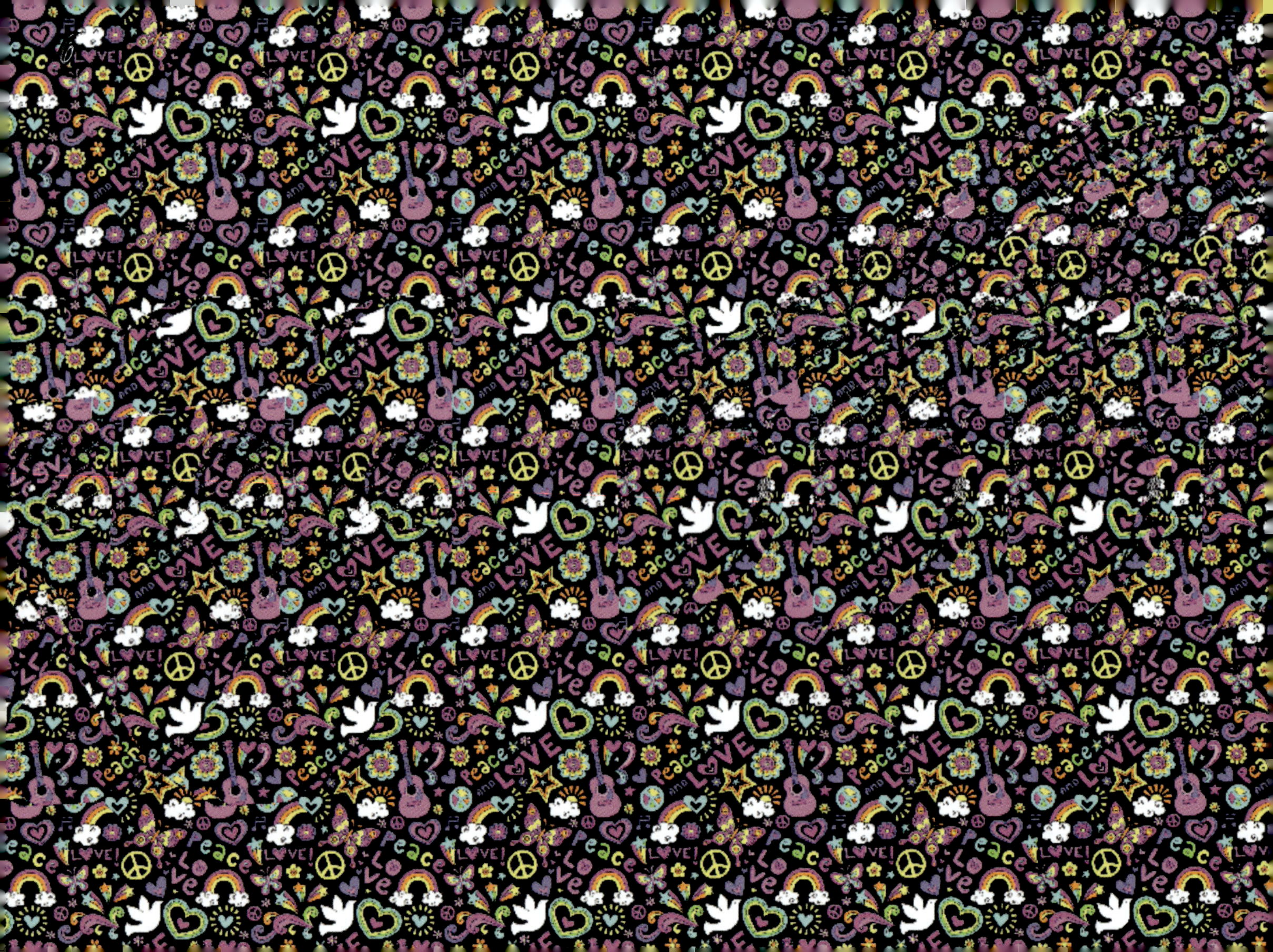
peace
LOVE!
peace and LOVE

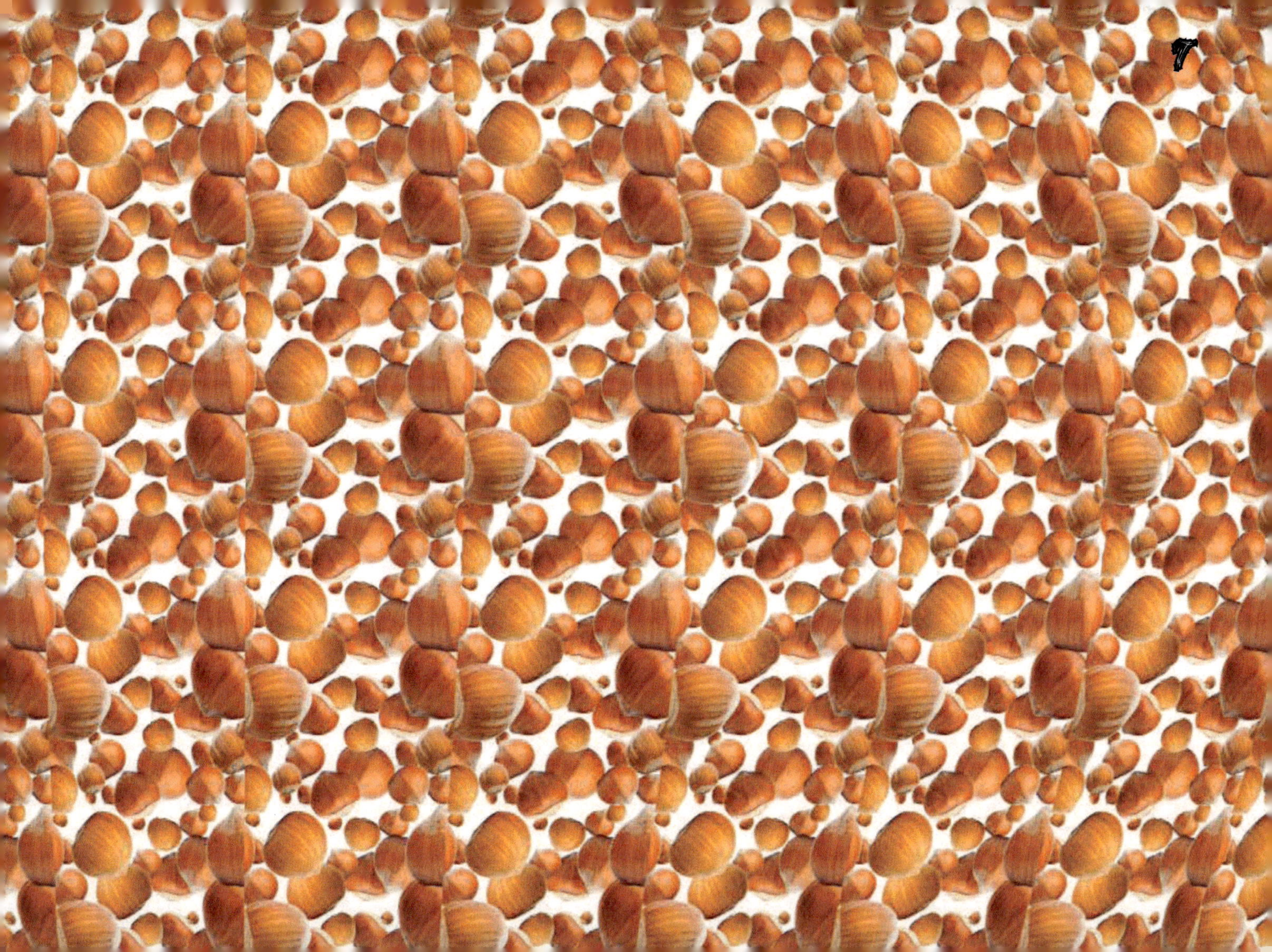

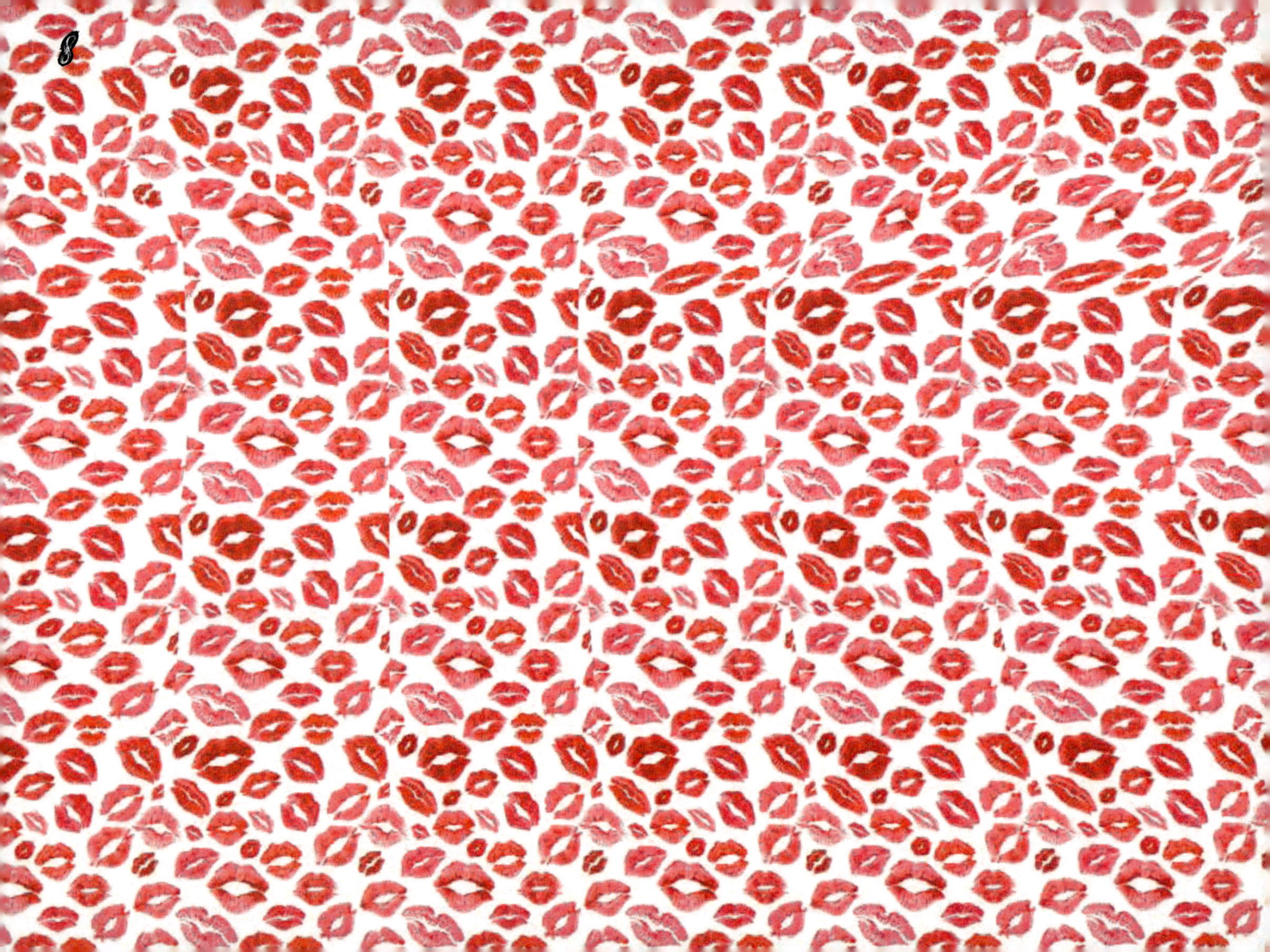

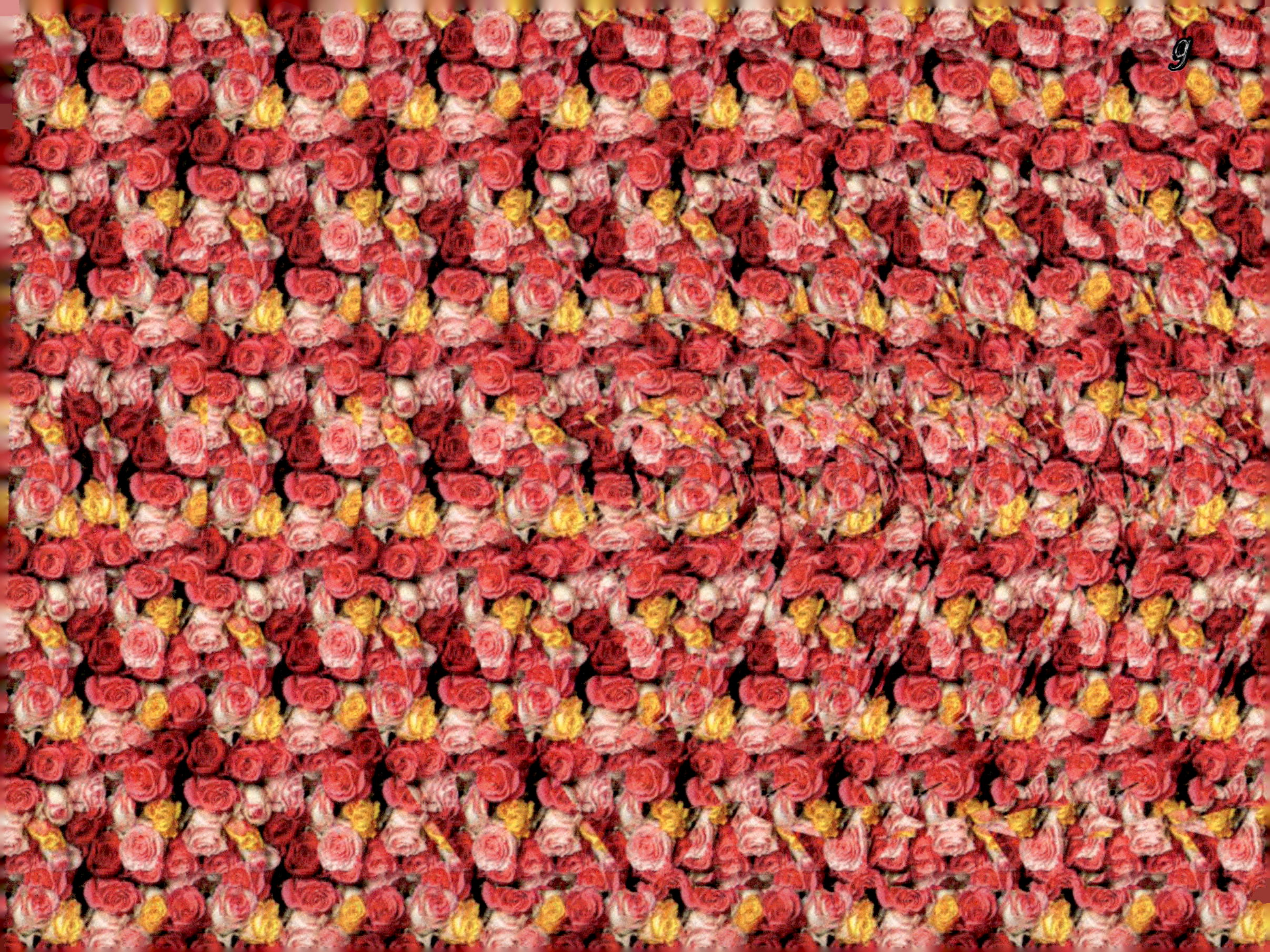

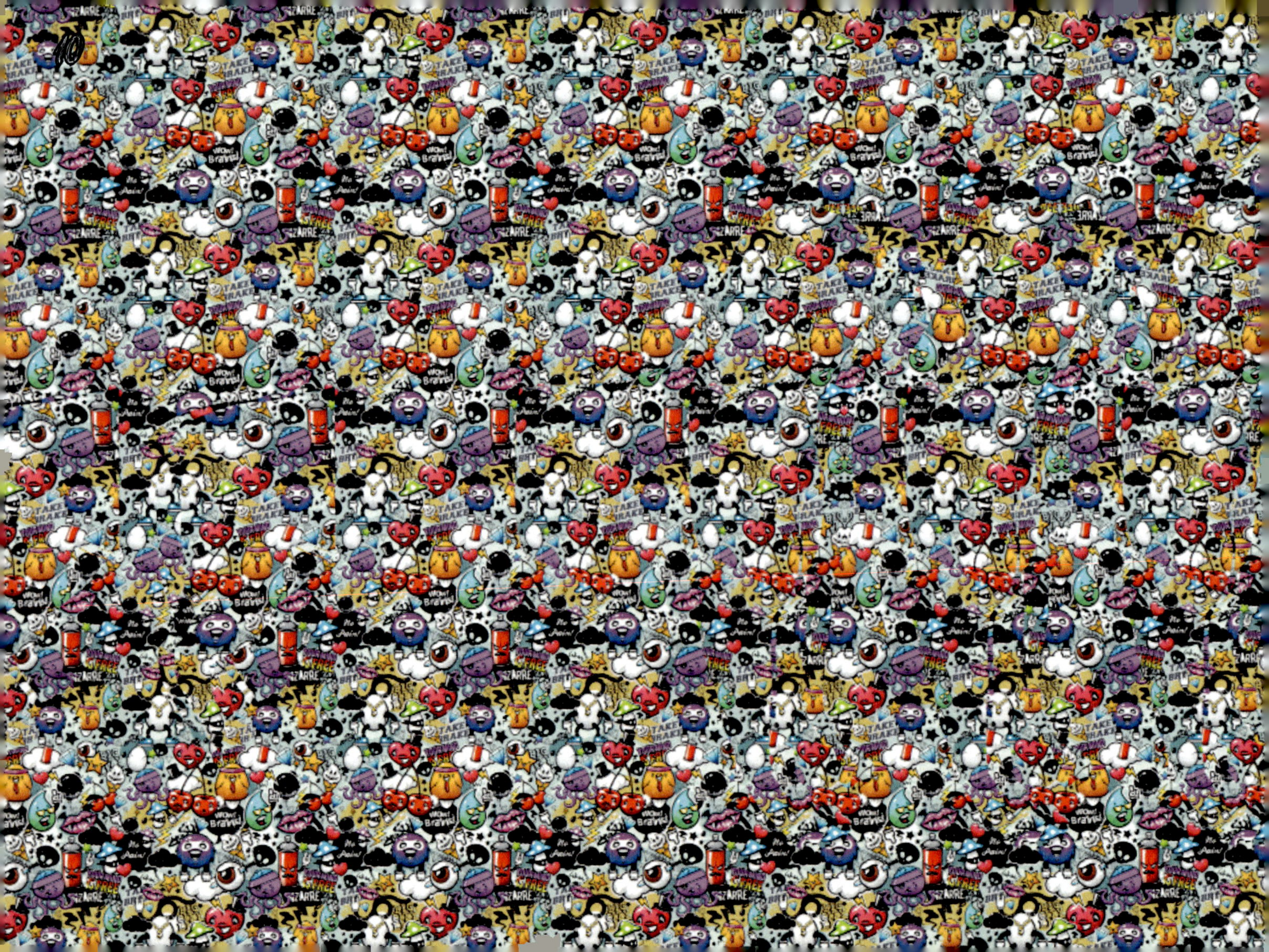

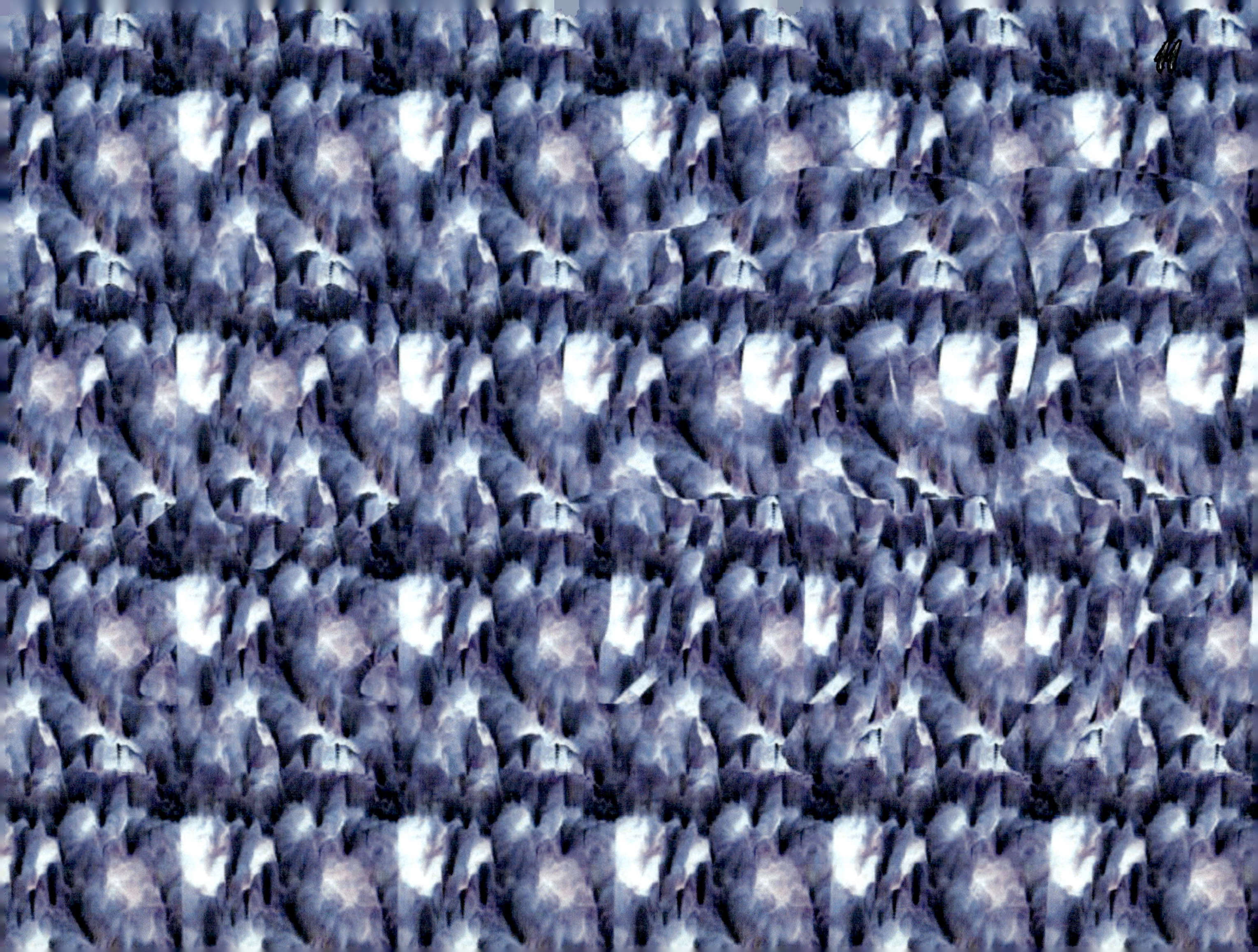

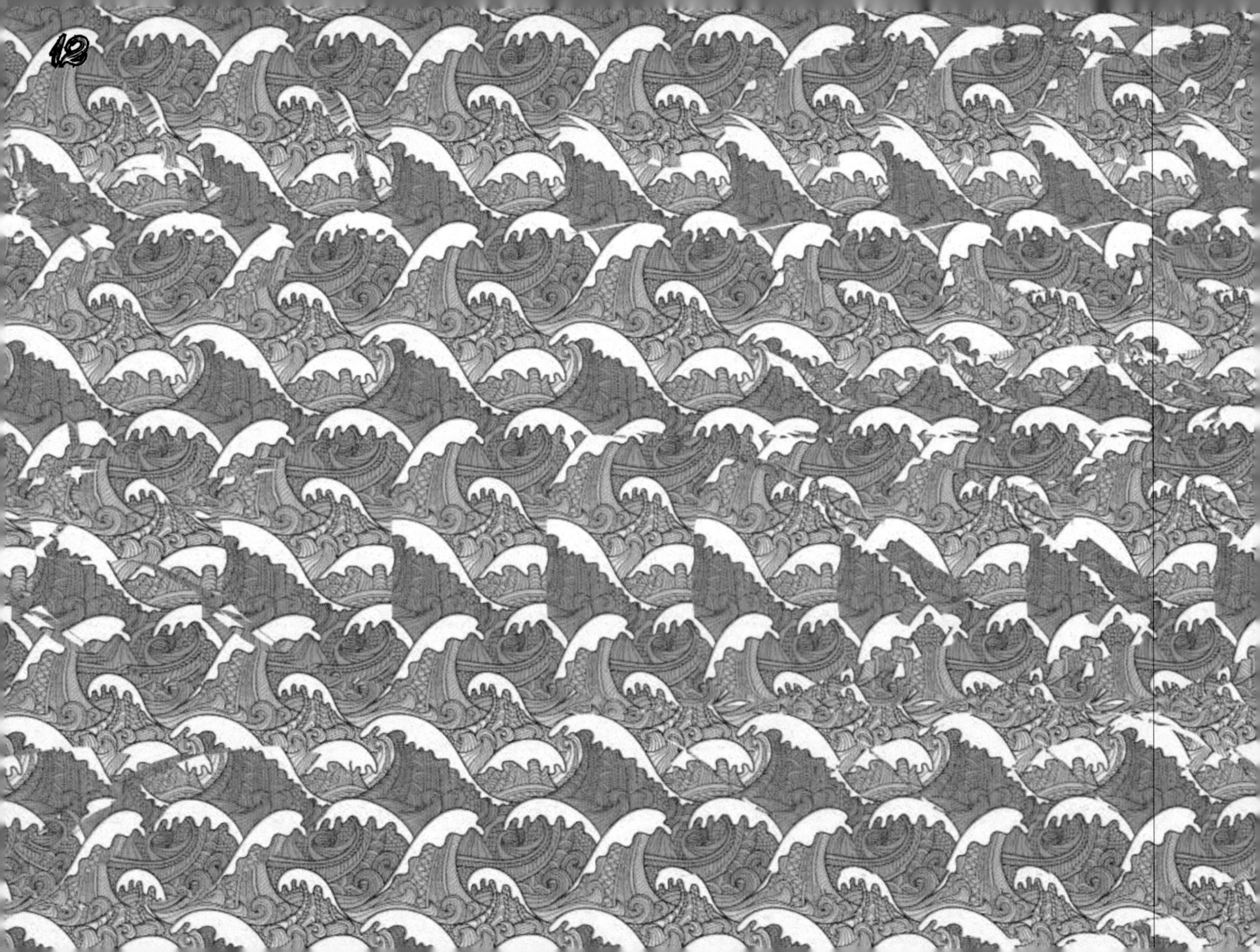

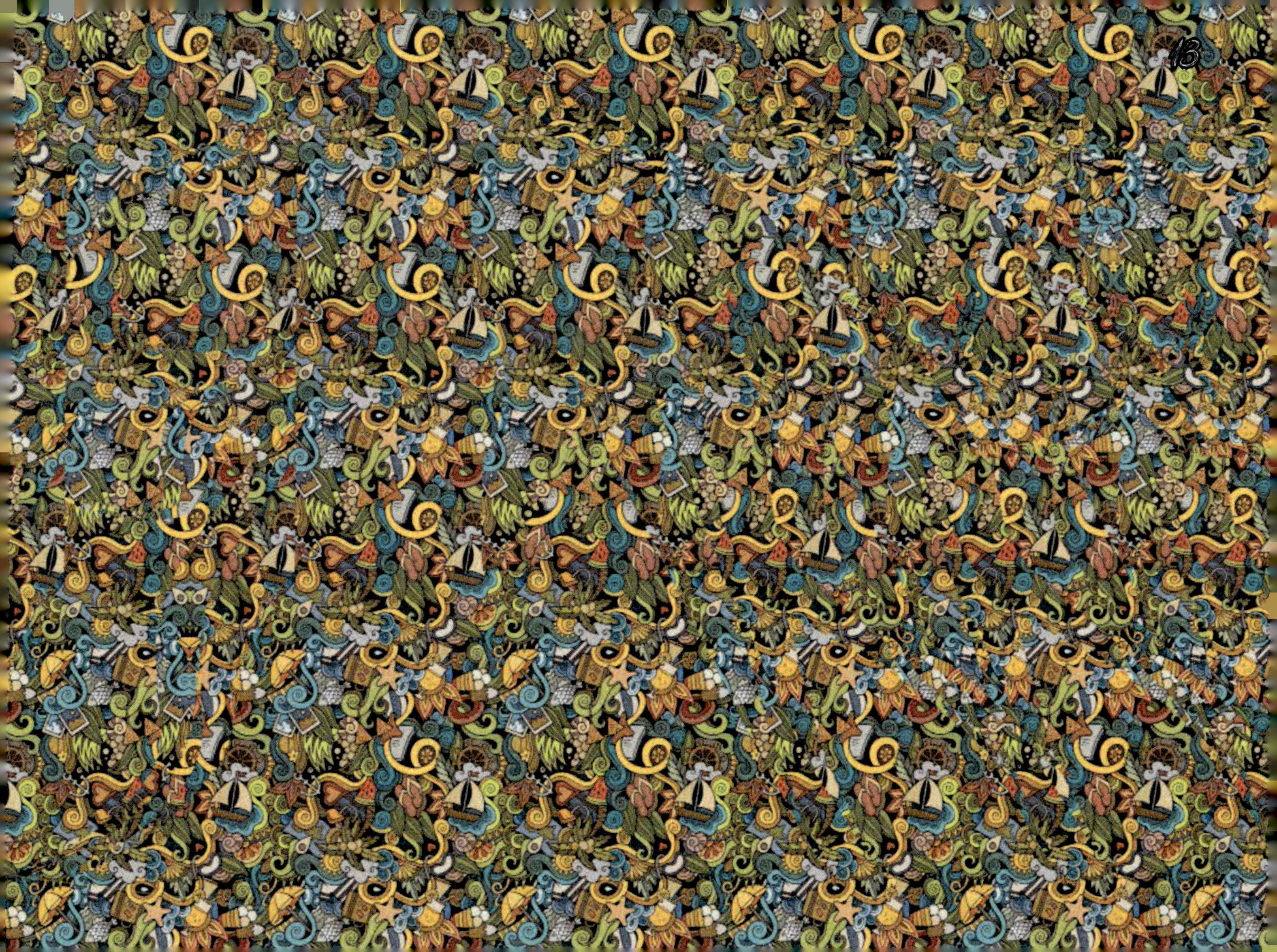

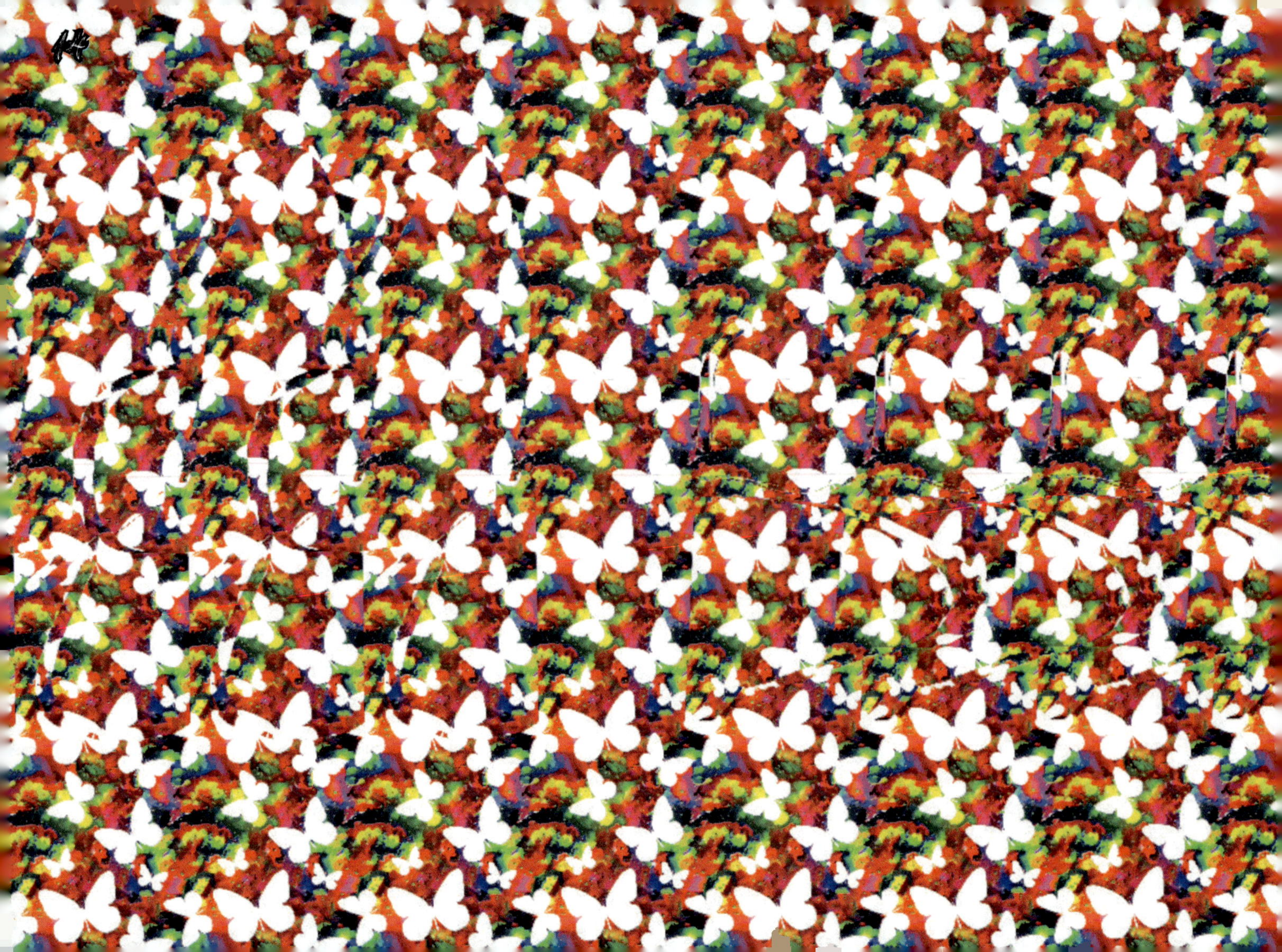

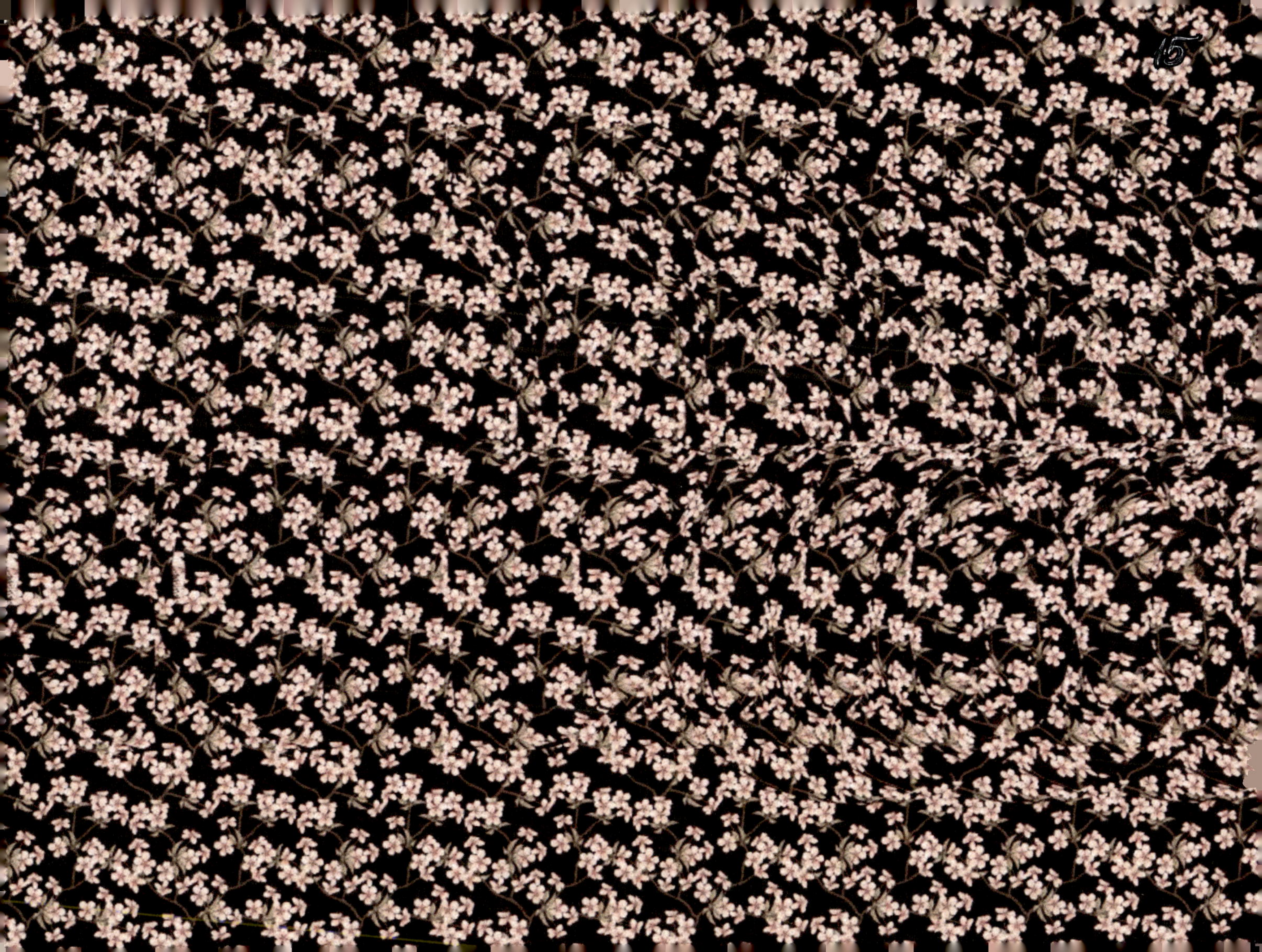

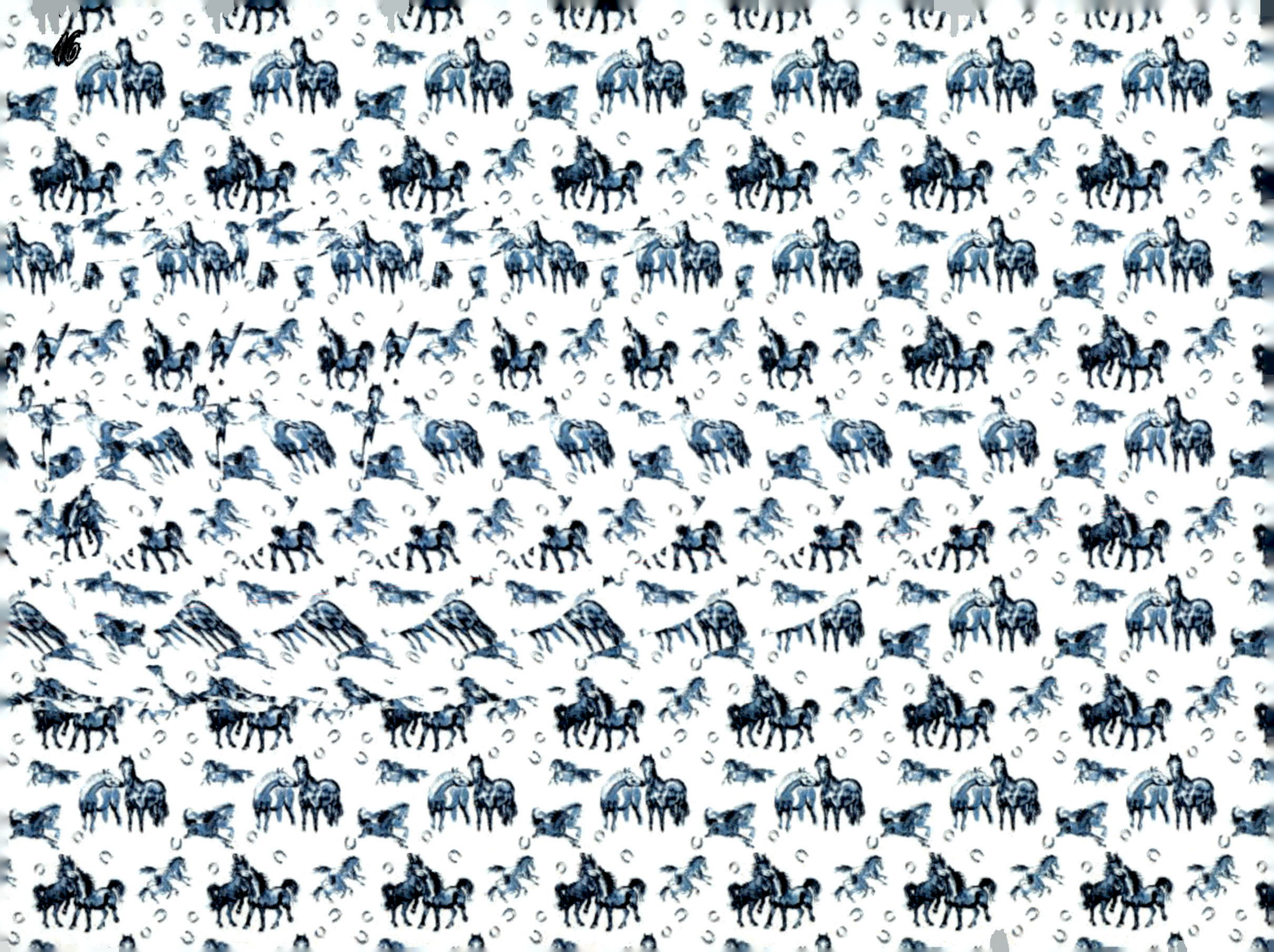

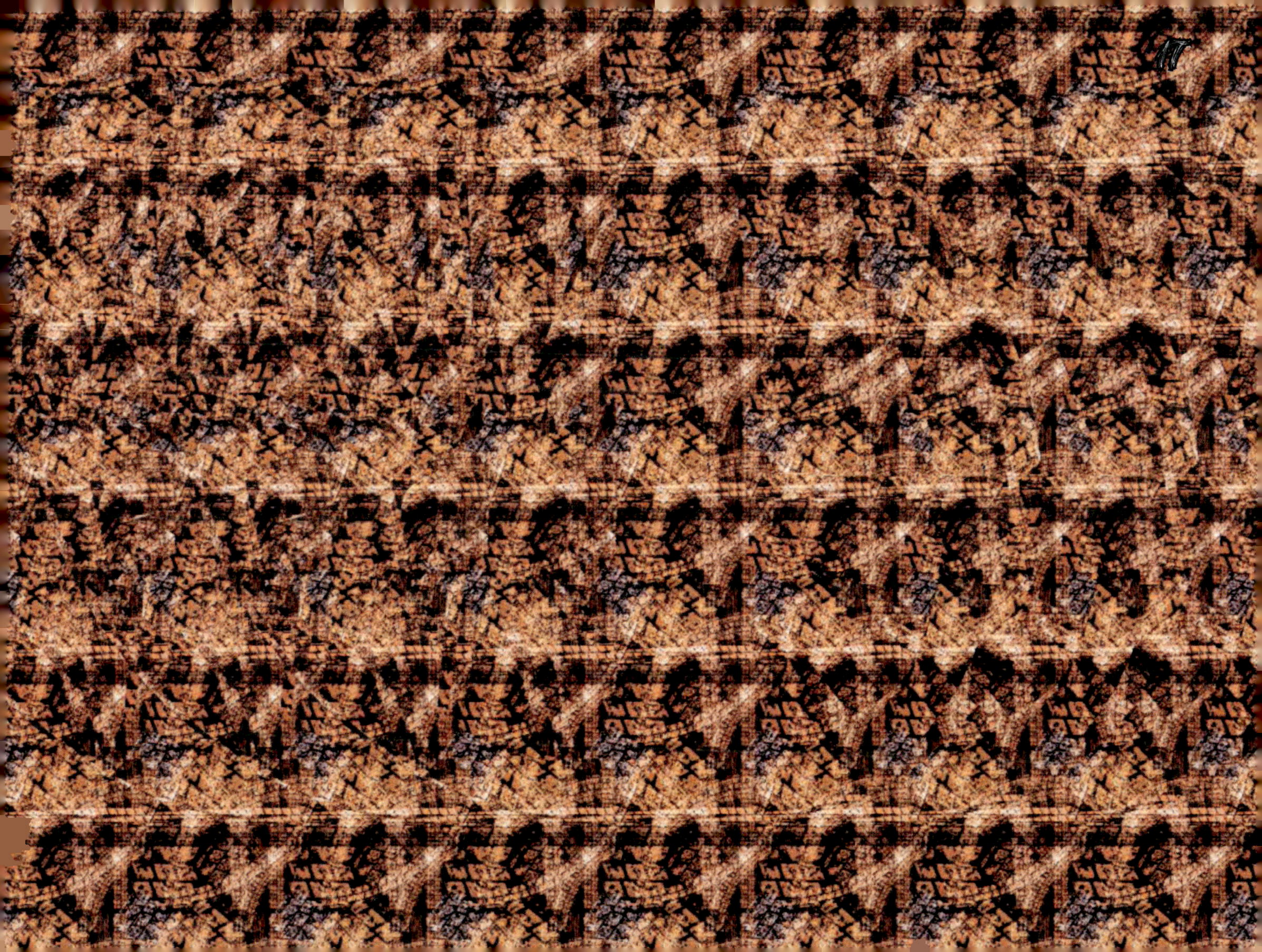

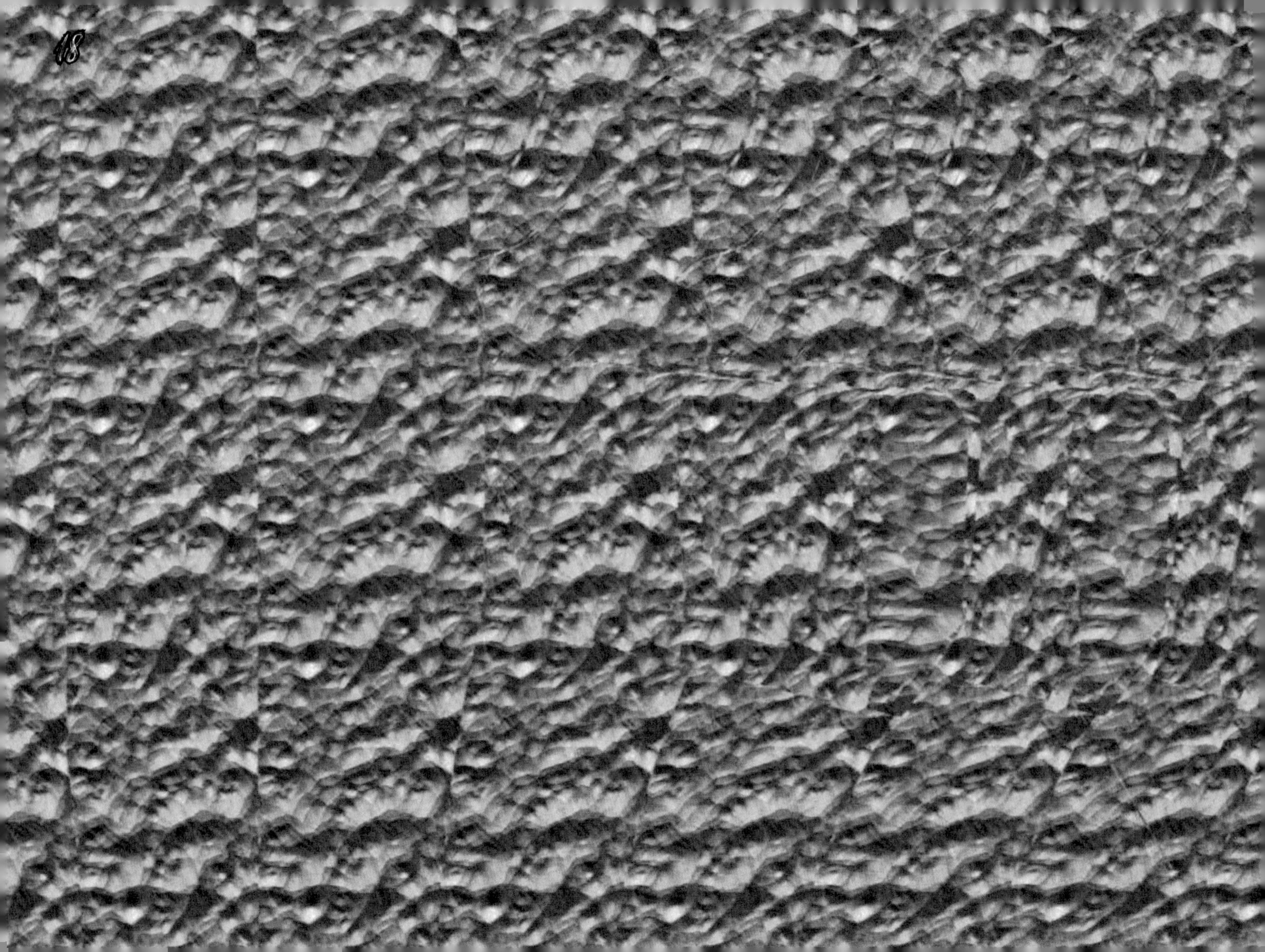

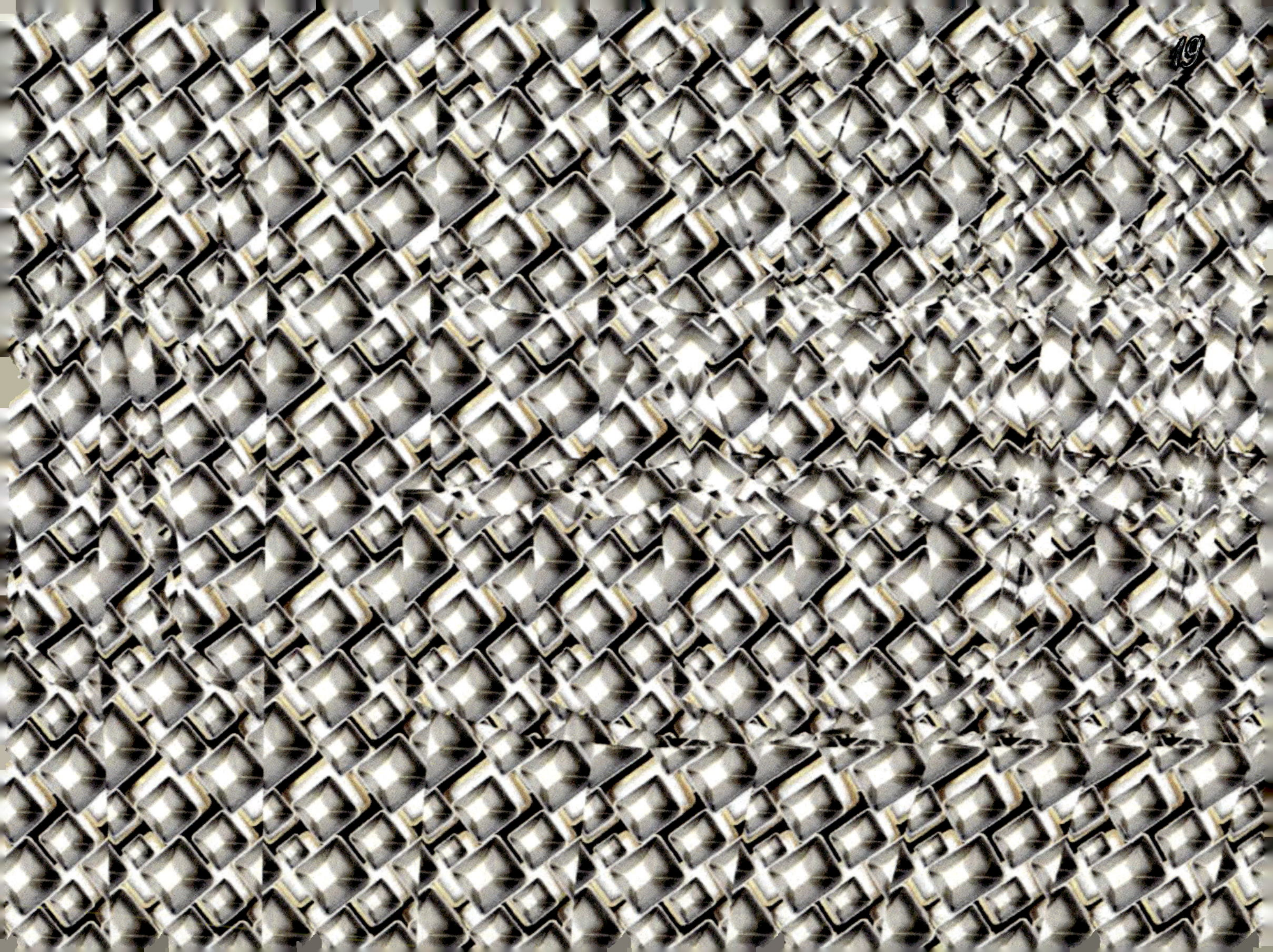

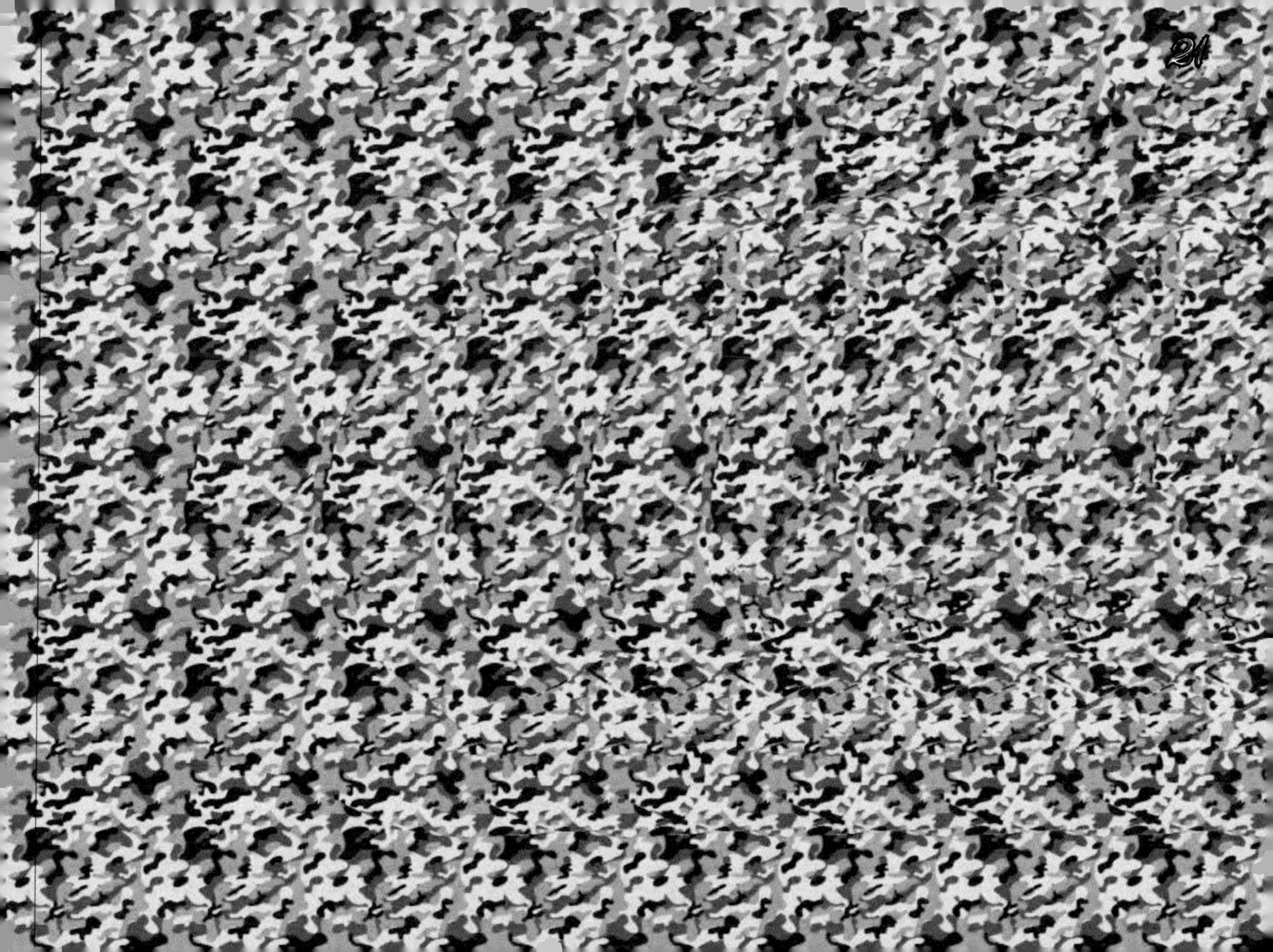

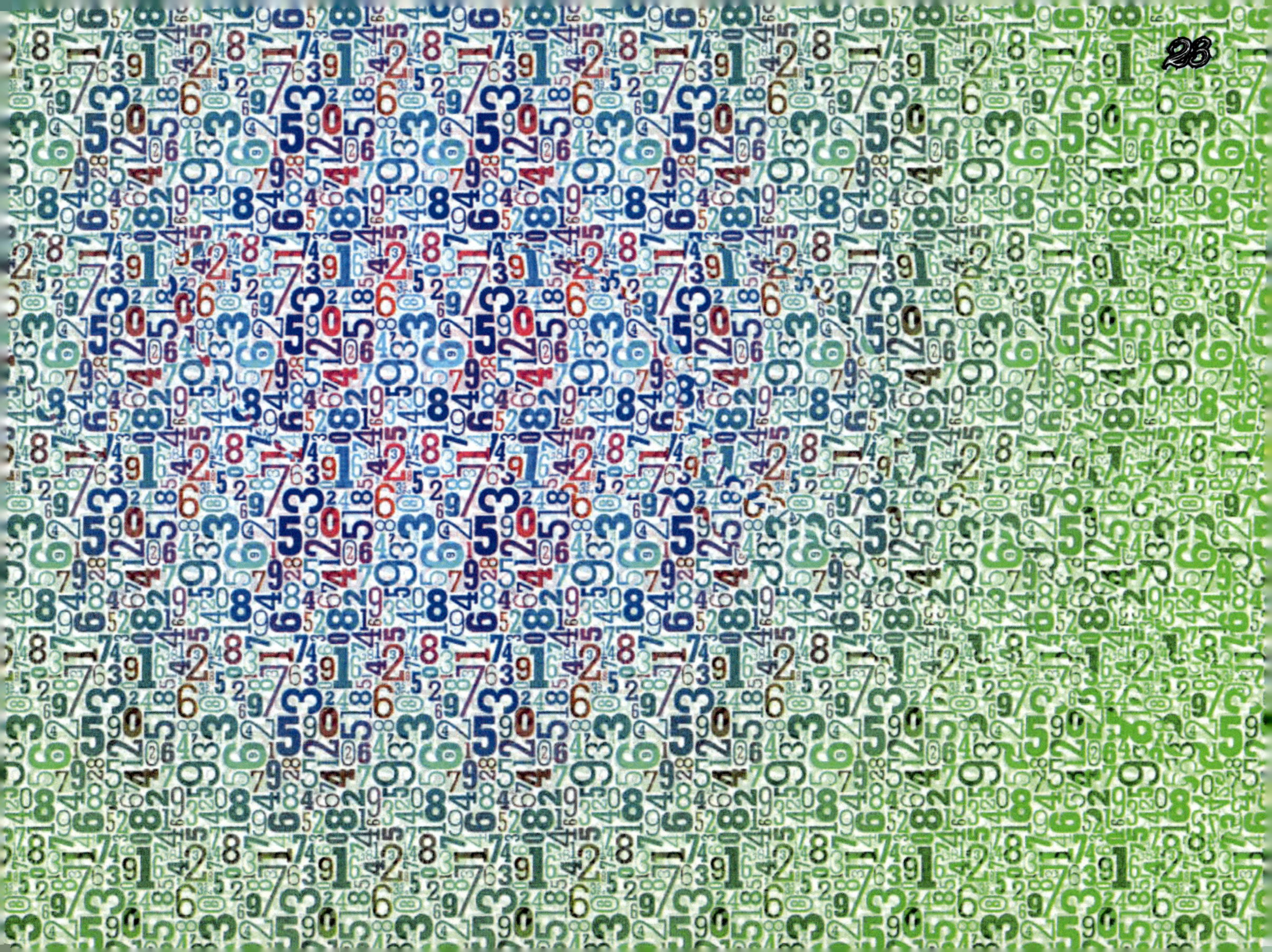

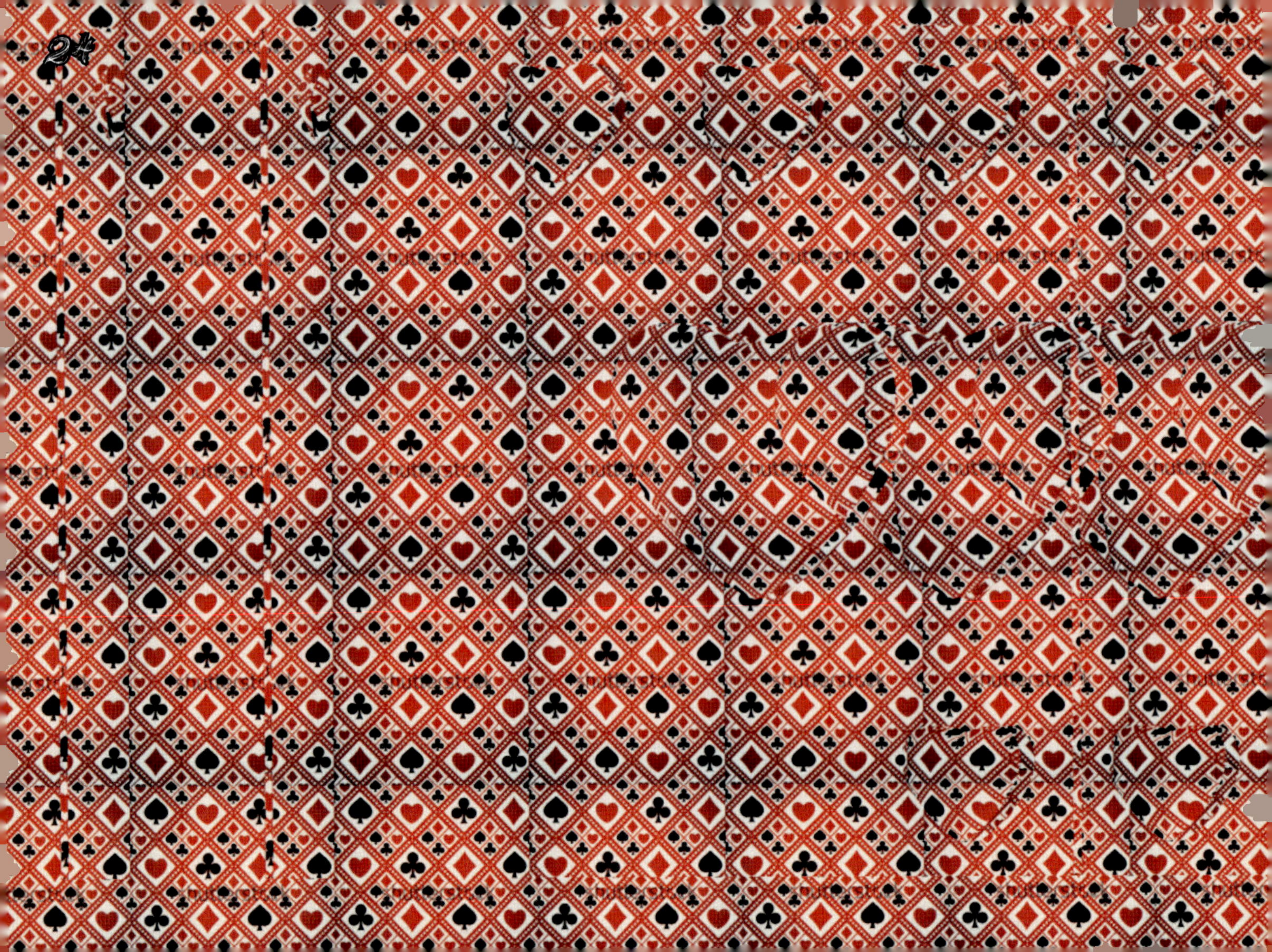

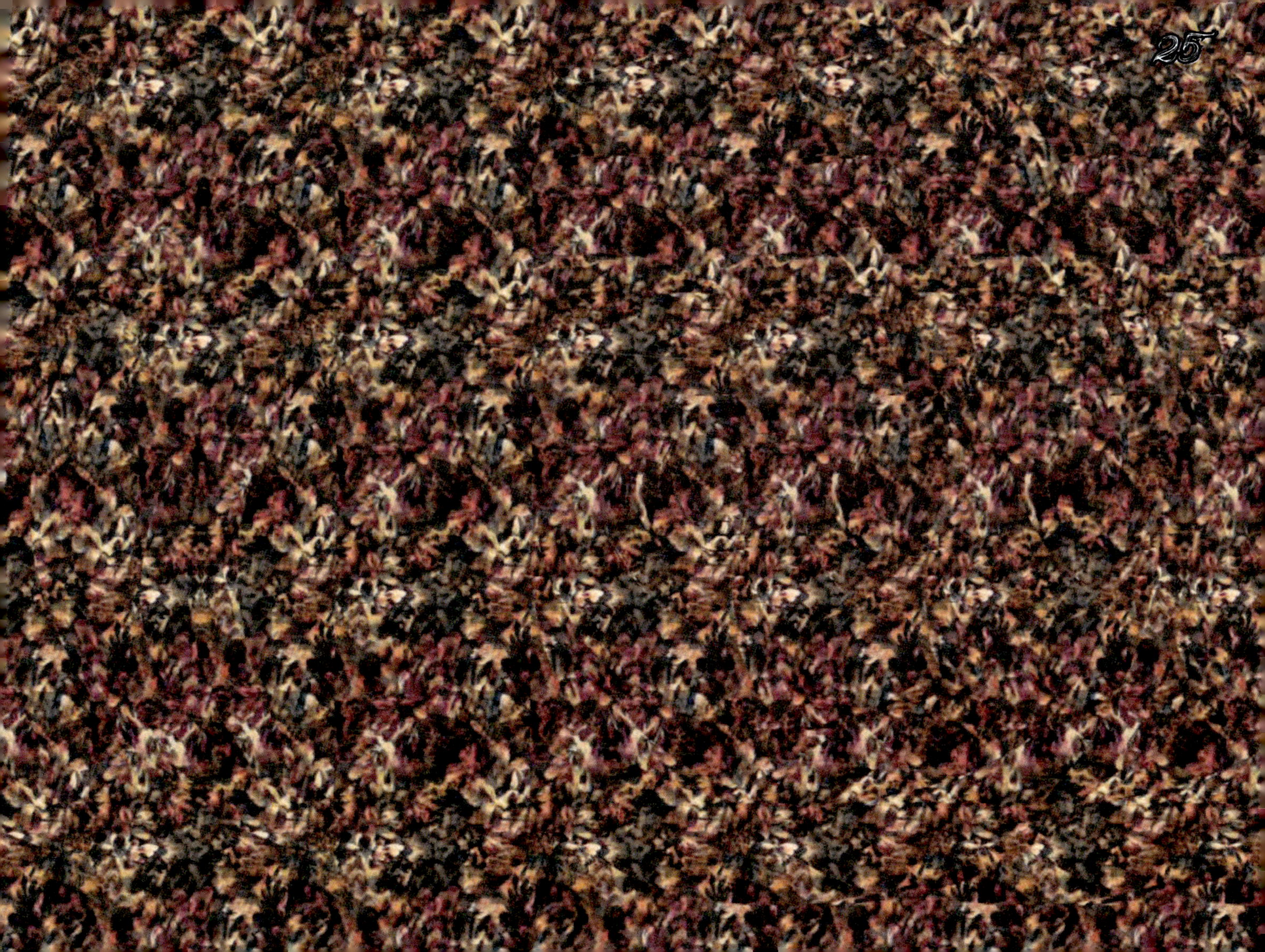

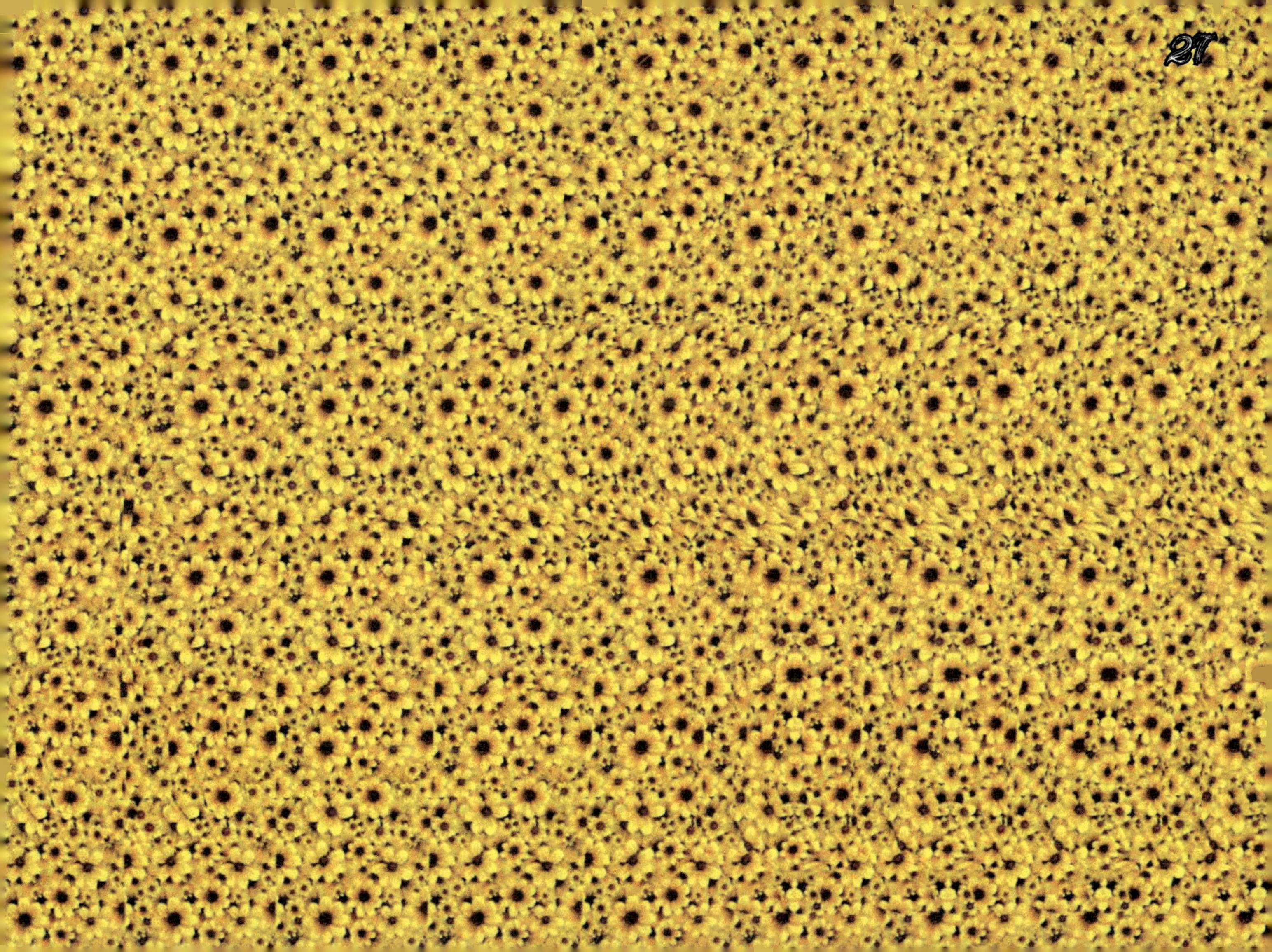

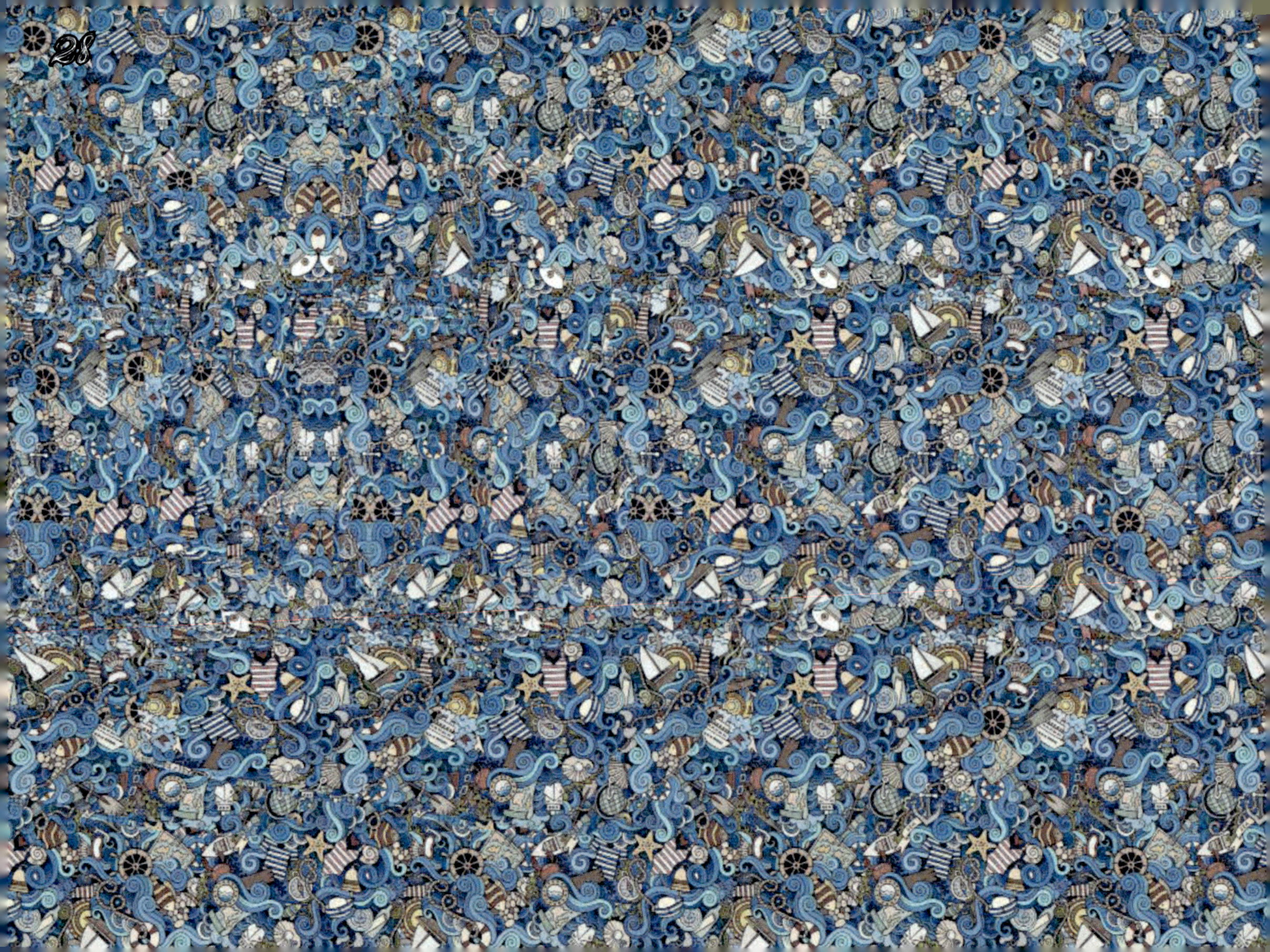

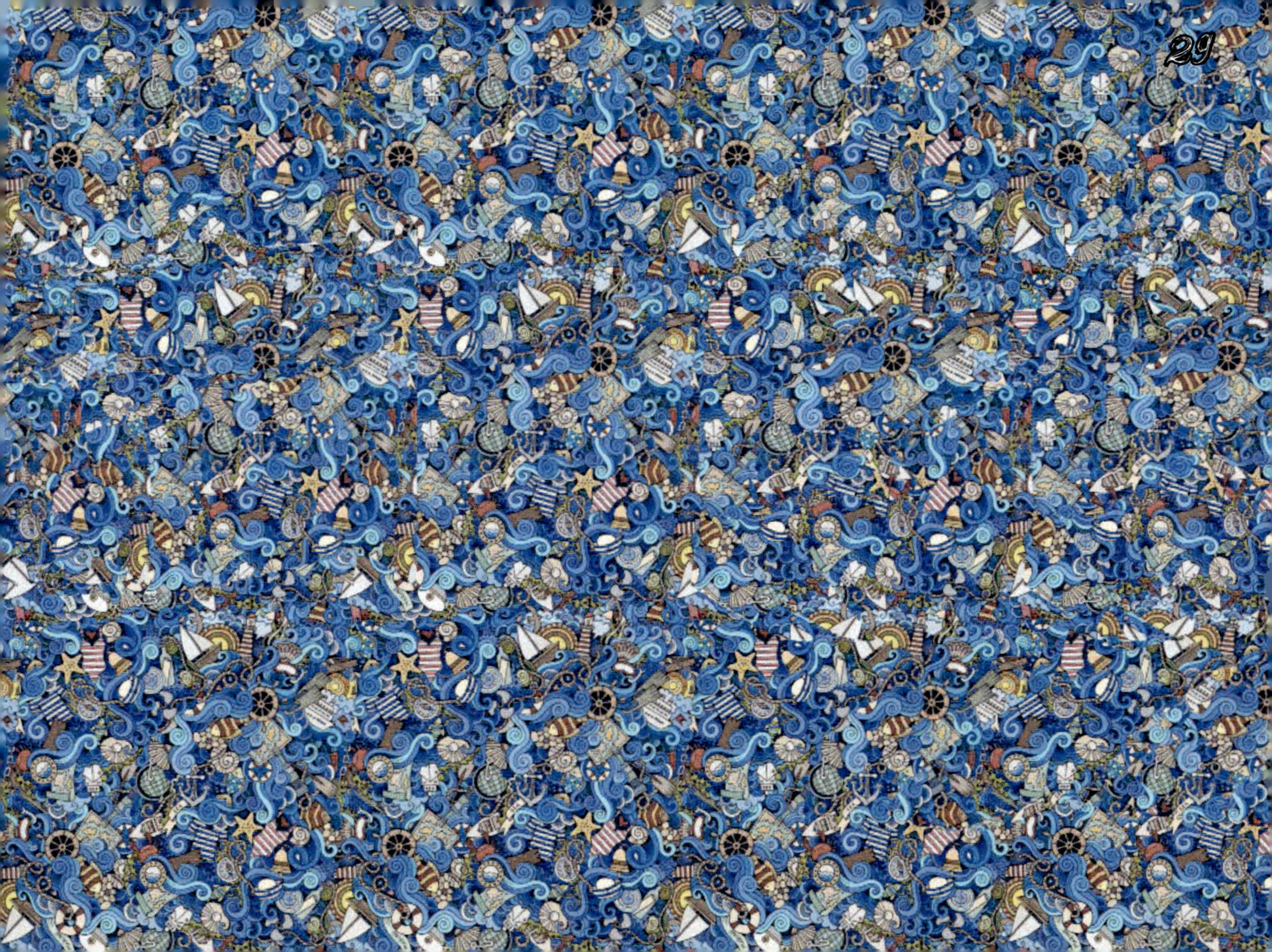

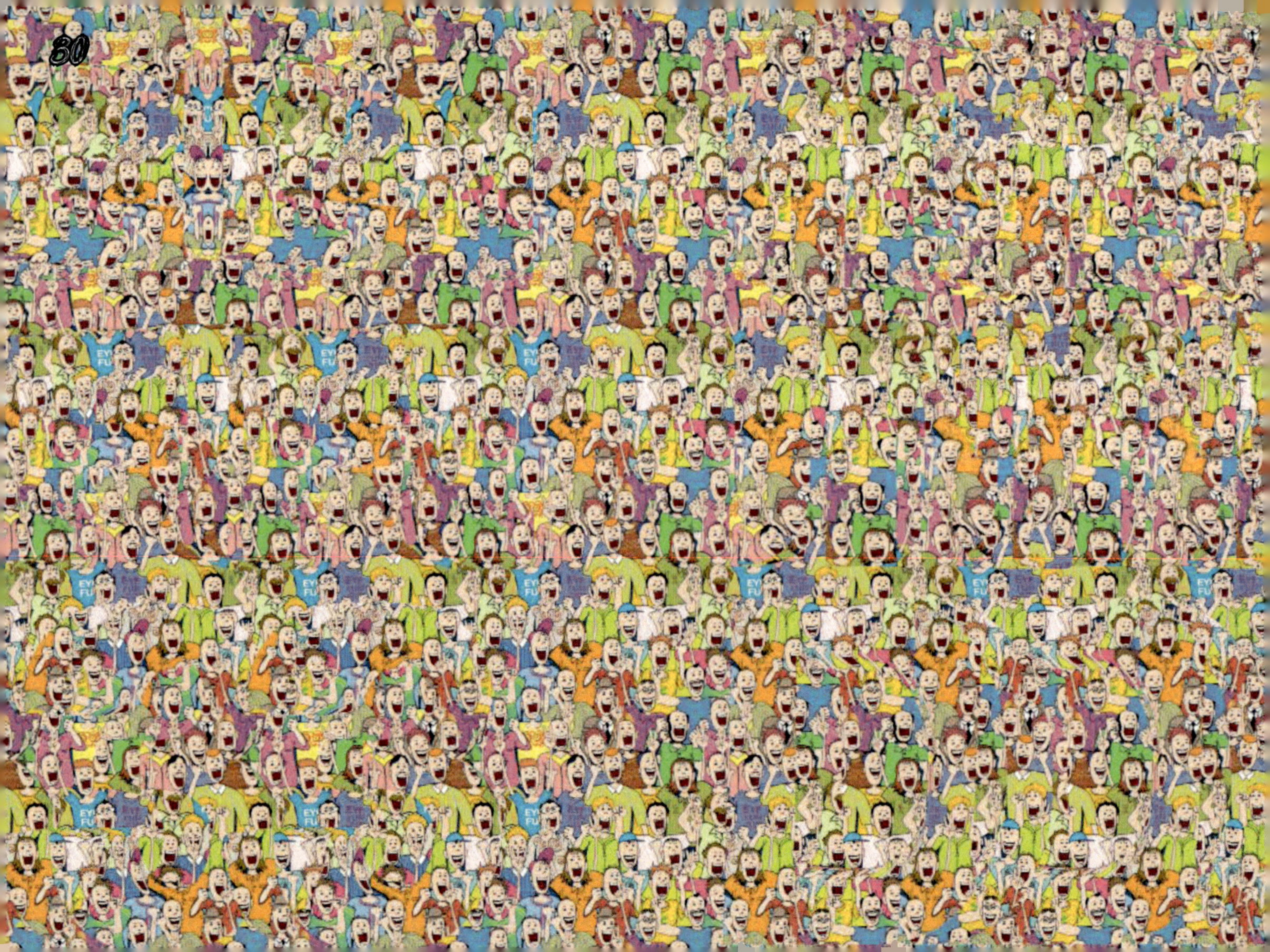

Publication of this edition: Allbit Publishing
Allbit Ltd Enterpirse Court Unit 4E Rotherham S63 5DB England

Creators and Authors: Steven Wilson, Marek Jacenko

ISBN: 978-1-940970-21-9

Contact for special editions, wholesale and corporate purchases:
go to the website eyefun3d.com

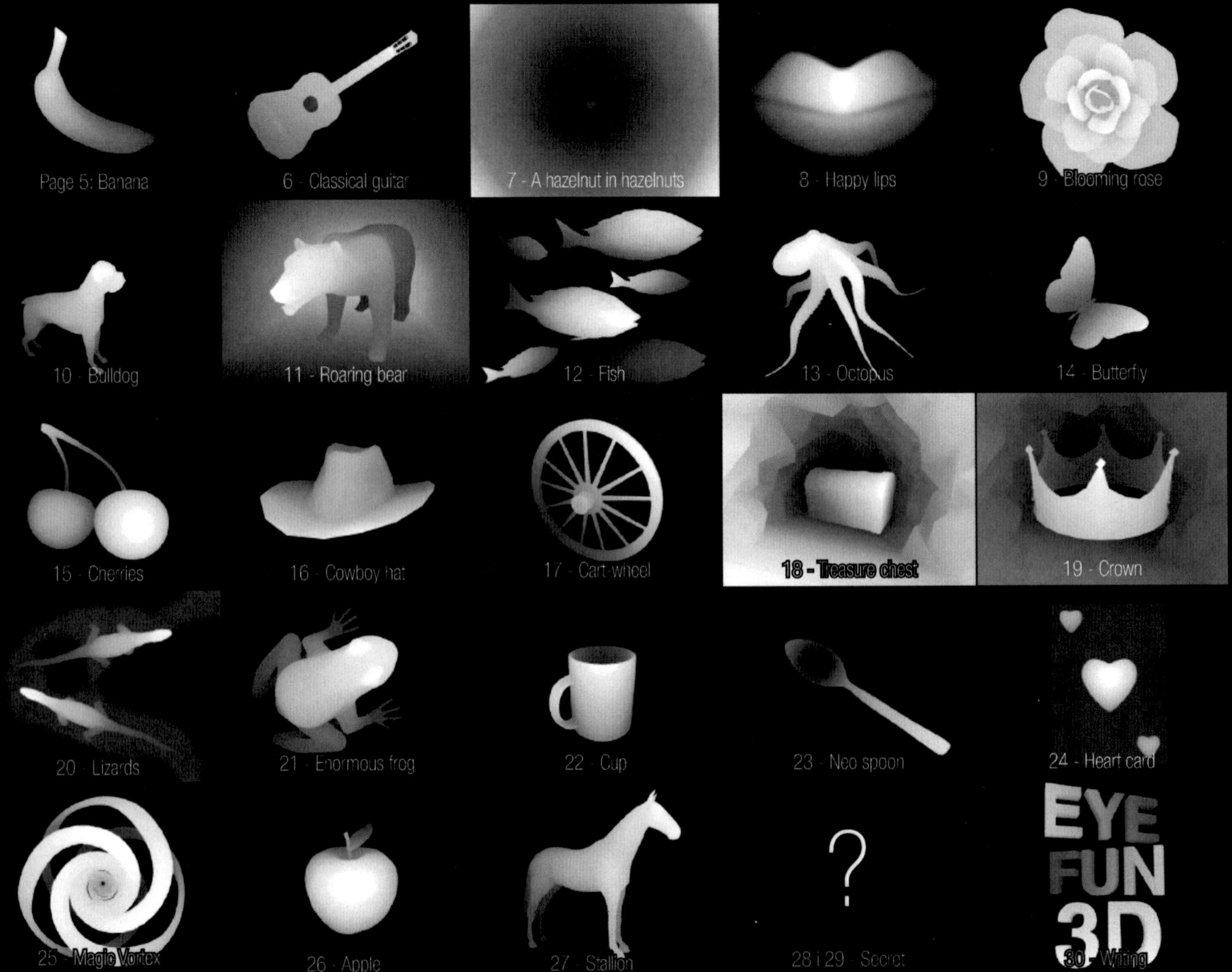
Page 5: Banana
6 - Classical guitar
7 - A hazelnut in hazelnuts
8 - Happy lips
9 - Blooming rose
10 - Bulldog
11 - Roaring bear
12 - Fish
13 - Octopus
14 - Butterfly
15 - Cherries
16 - Cowboy hat
17 - Cart-wheel
18 - Treasure chest
19 - Crown
20 - Lizards
21 - Enormous frog
22 - Cup
23 - Neo spoon
24 - Heart card
25 - Magic Vortex
26 - Apple
27 - Stallion
?
28 i 29 - Secret
EYE
FUN
3D
30 - Writing

Made in the USA
Middletown, DE
08 December 2023

45072404R00020